The author wishes to extend special thanks to all the interpreters at Old Sturbridge Village, Sturbridge, Massachusetts, for their invaluable assistance to him in the research for this book.

4th Grade

MW01097824

The Olden Days

A Random House PICTUREBACK®

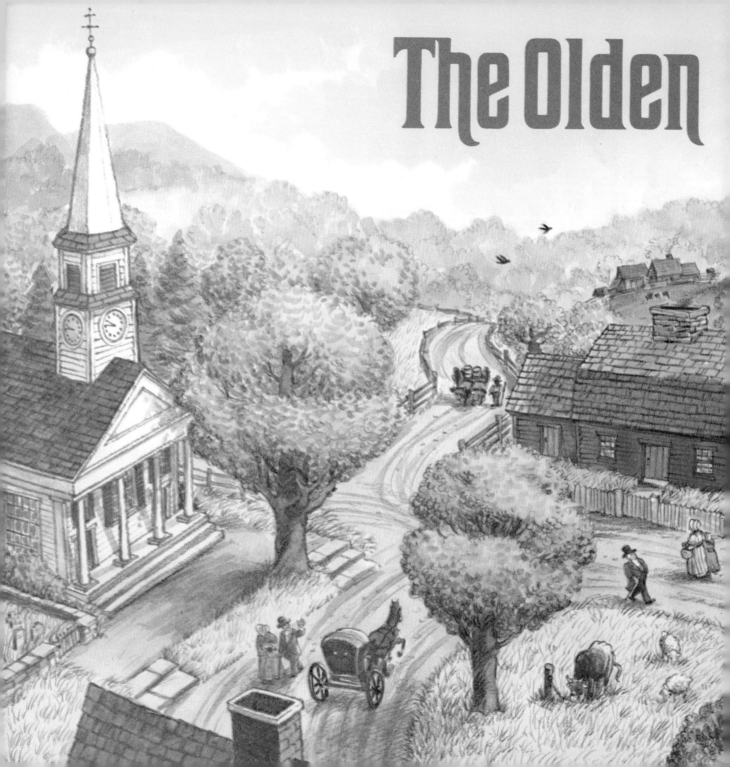

The Olden

Days

by Joe Mathieu

RANDOM HOUSE NEW YORK

What was it like in the olden days? About 150 years ago,
a New England village was a small, quiet place. There were
no cars or trucks on its dirt streets, and no airplanes flying
overhead. People rode from place to place on horseback or in
horse-drawn buggies. The village shops stood close together
around the common pasture, where people could leave their
horses and other animals to graze.

The general store was a lively shop. It stocked many things the villagers needed. There were buckets and barrels, crockery and cloth, shovels and lanterns, spices and soap. People often traded for things instead of paying for them with money. They brought in their own handmade goods or home-grown vegetables and eggs.

When wooden wheels were in need of repair, they were brought to the wheelwright's shop. The wheelwright made and fixed wooden wagon wheels for all the wagons and buggies in the village.

To make a wagon wheel, the wheelwright hammered wooden spokes into holes in the hub—the center of the wheel. Next he fitted sections of the wooden wheel around the spokes. Finally, he cut a larger hole in the center of the hub so the wheel would fit perfectly on the wagon's axle.

The blacksmith was a very strong man,
and he had a very important job. He kept
a fire burning all day to heat the iron
he used to make things. He pumped the big
bellows to keep the fire hot.

Using a hammer and an anvil, he shaped
the hot pieces of metal into hinges, chains,
hooks, kettles, nails, tools, and horseshoes.

The blacksmith also nailed the horseshoes onto the horses' hoofs. Iron shoes protect the hoofs. The blacksmith made sure that the shoes fit just right. Then the horse could walk easily and without pain.

Farmers brought their dried corn and other grains to the gristmill. There it was ground into flour or meal for bread, cakes, biscuits, and pies. The gristmill stood beside a stream, which provided water power to turn the big water wheel. The water wheel turned the large millstones inside the mill.

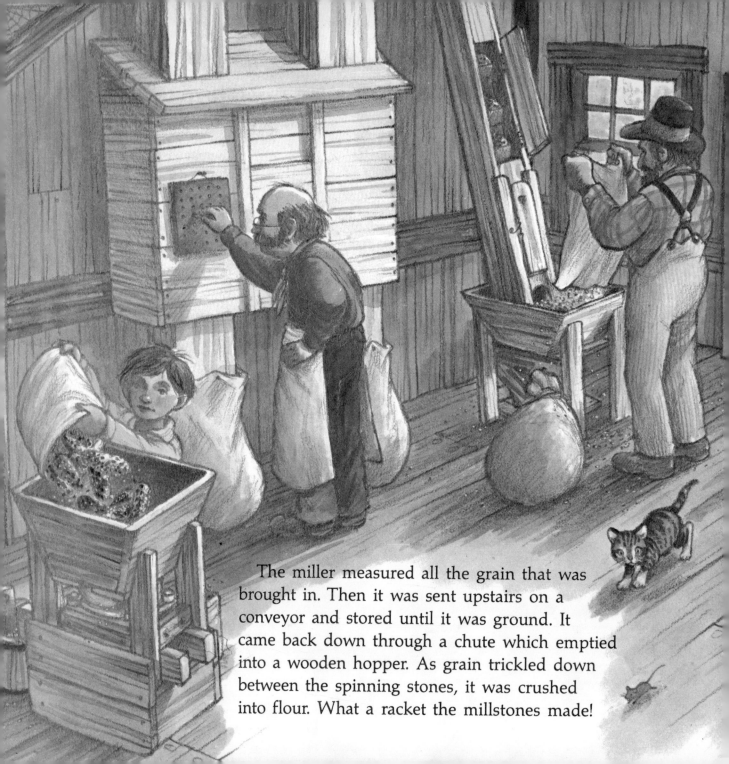

The miller measured all the grain that was
brought in. Then it was sent upstairs on a
conveyor and stored until it was ground. It
came back down through a chute which emptied
into a wooden hopper. As grain trickled down
between the spinning stones, it was crushed
into flour. What a racket the millstones made!

The carpenter's workshop was a busy place. The master carpenter made bedposts, and legs for chairs and tables on a machine called a lathe. His young apprentice turned the crank on the big wheel that ran the lathe. While the apprentice worked, he watched the carpenter carefully so he could learn the craft.

Carpenters made most of their own tools in the olden days. Many of them were much like the hand tools we use today. There were no electric machines for making furniture. A chair might take the carpenter many hours of hard work, but he always took great care. And he could be proud of every piece he made.

All the neighbors pitched in to help build a barn in the olden days. Some men cut down trees and some cut them into beams and boards. Some laid the boards down to make the floor. Others fitted and pounded the big beams together on the ground to make the barn's frame.

When the heavy sections of frame were finished, the men pushed them up into place with long wooden poles called pikes. They used wooden pegs instead of nails to hold the frame together.

A barn raising was a big event, and the women prepared a huge feast. Everyone was tired at the end of the day, but they had had a great time.

In the olden days the kitchen was the main room of the house. Its big fireplace was used for cooking as well as heating. Women carried their own firewood to keep the fire going all day. They cooked delicious meals in heavy iron pots and kettles. They grew their own vegetables and raised their own animals for meat. They made cider with apples from their own trees.

Girls helped their mothers with all the chores. What a hot and tiring job, turning the roast over the fire for hours!

The beehive oven was a part of the fireplace. Fresh bread was baked in it every day.

Most of the people were farmers in the olden days. And they made almost everything they needed. Farmers who raised sheep sheared their wool off every year for making cloth.

After the wool was washed, it was carded between two spiked boards to make it smooth. Then it was twisted into long strands of yarn on the spinning wheel. Afterwards it was colored with dyes made from leaves, berries, or bark.

It took lots of practice to learn how to weave on the big loom. Dyed yarn was woven into cloth for beautiful blankets, winter smocks, shawls, coats, and other clothing. In the olden days women made clothes for everyone in the family.

People didn't drink much milk
in the olden days. There were no
refrigerators to keep it fresh and
cold. Instead, women and girls
used milk to make butter in the
butter churn.

They also made cheese by
separating the solid part of the
milk, the curds, from the liquid
part, called the whey. Butter and
cheese were easier to store
without spoiling than milk.

There were no light bulbs in the olden days. People lit their homes with candles. Women made their own candles by dipping string wicks into melted animal fat over and over again.

Some women made home medicines by crushing and mixing dried herbs they had grown in their gardens.

The village schoolhouse had only one
room, and one schoolmaster taught all
of the children. They learned how to read,
write, and count. There were very few
books, and they were expensive. Most
pupils learned their numbers and alphabet
from a hornbook. It was a board protected
from wear by a thin sheet of clear horn.
The horn covered a piece of paper
with the letters and numbers printed on it.
Children practiced writing with chalk
on small black slates.

The last snow of the winter was
called the "sugar snow." That was the
season for making maple sugar. The men made
holes in the maple trees and put a spout in each
hole. They hung up buckets to catch the sap that dripped
out. The sap was boiled in a big iron pot to make maple syrup.
When they boiled off all the liquid, they got maple sugar.

In the olden days there were no furnaces to keep the houses snug and warm. At bedtime mothers warmed the cold sheets with a bed warmer filled with hot coals from the fireplace.

The children were tucked into their trundle bed, which pulled out from under their parents' bed. And that's what life was like in the olden days.